BY VEGAN SOUL FOODIE RECIPE GUIDE: DISHES SO DECADENT YOU CAN SERVE TO MEAT LOVERS.

For more, books, classes, sales, and videos visit our website by using this QR Code.

Vegan Soul Foodie Recipe Guide: DISHES SO DECADENT YOU CAN SERVE TO MEAT LOVERS.

© Brooke Brimm Ministries

🌐 www.vegansoulfoodie.com
📷 instagram.com/vegan.soulfoodie
f facebook.com/groups/vegansoulfood

© Brooke Brimm Ministries

FRIED THINGS — 6
Buffalo Cauliflower — 7
Buffalo tofu po' boys — 9
Hot Chicken Fried Oyster Mushrooms — 11
Fried hearts of palm calamari — 13
Portabella Mushroom Cheesesteak Egg Rolls — 14

FINGER FOODS — 15
Spinach-Stuffed Mushrooms — 16
Garlic Butter "Salmon" Cakes — 17
Spinach in the blanket — 18
"Cheesesteak" sliders — 19
Sweet Glazed Meatballs — 21

SANDWICHES — 22
Chopped Cheese Sandwich — 23
Vegan Sloppy Burger — 24
UnTuna Salad Melt Sandwich — 26
Portabella "Beef n' Cheddar" Sandwich — 28

DESSERTS — 29
Sweet potato pie — 30
Huckleberry Cobbler — 31
Maple Banana Bread — 32
Banana Ice Cream — 33
Cranberry & Apple Sauce — 34

BREADS 35
Skillet Cornbread 36
Vegan "Honey" buttermilk biscuits 37

SIDES 38
Turnip Greens 39
Garlic Broccoli 40
Corn pudding 41
Fried Cabbage and Potatoes 42
Black Beans and Rice 43
Stewed Okra, Corn, & Tomatoes 44
Sweet Potato Soufflé 45

ENTREES 46
Salisbury Steak 47
Gyro Salad 49
Vegan Chili 51
Vegan Oxtails 52
Egg Foo Young 54
Jackfruit Pot Pie 56
Beyond Vegan Ribs 58

FRIED FOOD

Fried food is fun. Most people do not hate fun, so why hate fried foods? Enjoy yourself. Indulge. You do not have to have fried foods everyday, but definitely treat yourself to some fried goodness.

The plus is that these fried yummies are made from plants, so you will be taking in less calories. You will also be getting fiber and nutrients such as Vitamin D, protein, and iron.

Crunch on this crispy goodness and celebrate in your heart and soul!

BUFFALO CAULIFLOWER

Ingredients

Wet Batter
1 cup all-purpose flour
1 cup water (more or less)
1 tsp onion powder
1 tsp garlic powder
1 tsp sea salt
1 tsp of mushroom seasoning

Dry Batter
1 cup all-purpose flour
1 tsp onion powder
1 tsp garlic powder
1 tsp smoked paprika

Buffalo Sauce
1 cup of hot sauce
½ cup of vegan butter or plant margarine
1 tsp of garlic powder
1 tsp onion powder
1/4 tsp of black pepper
1 tsp agave nectar or maple syrup

Vegan Ranch Dressing
1 cup of vegan mayonnaise
Juice of 1 lemon
½ jalapeño stemmed, deseeded, and minced
3 TBSPs of cilantro, chopped
1/8 cup nutritional yeast
1/8 cup unflavored and unsweetened plant
milk Salt and pepper to taste

One raw head of Cauliflower

Instructions

1. Cut cauliflower into bite size pieces.

2. Whisk together wet batter ingredients, it should be the consistency of pancake batter. Evenly coat cauliflower bites with it.

3. Add dry batter ingredients into a plastic bag. Drop wet battered cauliflower into the bag of dry batter and shake until well coated.

4. Deep fry cauliflower in vegetable oil or spray them with oil and air fry them. When light golden brown, drain onto a paper towel.

5. Melt butter on the stove and add hot sauce, garlic powder, onion powder, pepper, and agave nectar.

6. Toss cauliflower in hot sauce mixture.

7. Serve with vegan ranch dressing and celery sticks.

BUFFALO TOFU PO' BOYS

Ingredients

1 box of extra firm tofu, crumbled into bite sized pieces
1/8 cup Tamari sauce or liquid aminos
1 TBSP garlic powder
1 cup of vegetable oil for frying
1 large french bread roll or four small french rolls
5 leaves of Romaine lettuce or a handful of mixed greens
1 medium tomato sliced

Wet Batter
1 cup all-purpose flour
1 cup water (more or less)
1 tsp onion powder
1 tsp garlic powder
1 tsp sea salt
1 tsp of mushroom seasoning

Dry Batter
1 cup all-purpose flour
1 tsp onion powder
1 tsp garlic powder
1 tsp smoked paprika

Buffalo Sauce
1 cup of hot sauce
½ cup of vegan butter or plant margarine
1 tsp of garlic powder
1 tsp onion powder
1/4 tsp of black pepper
1 tsp agave nectar or maple syrup

Vegan Ranch Dressing
1 cup of vegan mayonnaise
Juice of 1 lemon
½ jalapeño stemmed, deseeded, and minced
3 TBSPs of cilantro, chopped
1/8 cup nutritional yeast
1/8 cup unflavored and unsweetened plant milk
Salt and pepper to taste

Instructions

1. Crumble extra firm tofu into bite size pieces.

2. Marinade it in Tamari sauce and garlic powder for about 10 minutes.

3. Whisk together wet batter ingredients it should be the consistency of pancake batter & evenly coat tofu bites.

4. Add dry batter ingredients into a plastic bag. Drop wet battered tofu into the bag of dry batter and shake until well coated.

5. Deep fry tofu in vegetable oil or spray with oil and air fry them. When golden brown, drain onto a paper towel.

6. Melt butter on the stove and add hot sauce, garlic powder, onion powder, pepper, and agave nectar.

7. Toss tofu in hot sauce mixture.

8. Split open French bread, dig out the soft bread filling and leave the crusty shell.

9. Arrange a layer of lettuce and sliced tomato onto the bread.

10. Arrange buffalo tofu on top.

11. Drizzle vegan ranch dressing on top. Serve and enjoy.

HOT CHICKEN FRIED OYSTER MUSHROOMS

Ingredients

1 cup of vegetable oil more or less for frying
1 package oyster mushrooms. Most Asian markets sell them

Wet Batter
1 cup all-purpose flour
1 cup water (more or less)
1 tsp onion powder
1 tsp garlic powder
1 tsp sea salt
1 tsp of cajun or creole seasoning
1 tsp of mushroom seasoning

Dry Batter
1 cup flour
1 tsp onion powder
1 tsp garlic powder
1 tsp smoked paprika
1 tsp cajun or creole seasoning
1 tsp of dried parsley

Spicy Oil
½ cup vegetable oil
4 TBSP cayenne pepper
2 TBSP brown sugar
1 TBSP paprika
1 tsp garlic powder
1 tsp chili powder
1 tsp. sea salt

Instructions

1. Break oyster mushroom into bite size pieces.

2. Whisk together wet batter ingredients it should be the consistency of pancake batter. Evenly coat mushroom pieces.

3. Add dry batter ingredients into a plastic bag. Drop wet battered mushroom into the bag of dry batter and shake until well coated.

4. Deep fry mushrooms in vegetable oil or spray with oil and air fry them. When golden brown, drain onto a paper towel.

5. On the stove combine spicy oil ingredients.

6. Toss oyster mushroom in spicy oil mixture.

7. Drain and serve.

FRIED HEARTS OF PALM CALAMARI

Ingredients

1 can of hearts of palm, sliced into ringlets
1 cup of vegetable oil for frying

Wet Batter
1 cup all-purpose flour
1 cup water (more or less)
1 tsp onion powder
1 tsp garlic powder
1 tsp sea salt
1 tsp of cajun or creole seasoning
1 tsp of mushroom seasoning
1 Nori sheet, ground into dust or 4 tsp of Nori Komi Furikake,

Dry Batter
1 cup corn meal
1/4 cup of all-purpose flour
1 tsp onion powder
1 tsp garlic powder
1 tsp smoked paprika
1 tsp cajun or creole seasoning
1 tsp of dried parsley
2 tsp of Old Bay Seasoning

Instructions

1. In a bowl, mix wet batter.

2. Place hollow ringlet hearts of palm into wet mixture and coat well.

3. Mix dry batter ingredients together in a plastic bag. Drop wet hearts of palm ringlet into the dry mixture and shake.

4. Fry in oil or spray with oil and air fry them in your air fryer. Serve with cocktail sauce and enjoy.

PORTABELLA MUSHROOM CHEESESTEAK EGG ROLLS

Ingredients

Steak
2 large Portabellas sliced & then chopped
1 medium onion, sliced & them chopped
1 TBSP vegetable oil
S&P to taste

Cheese
2 potatoes, peeled & roughly chopped
1 small onion, roughly chopped
2 small carrots, roughly chopped
3 garlic cloves
1/4 cup raw cashews
1 poblano pepper
1 cup water
1/4 cup nutritional yeast

Vegan egg roll wrappers

1-2 cups of oil for deep frying.

Instructions

1. Sauté seasoned mushrooms & onions for 25 -30 mins in a oiled pan on medium heat.

2. Boil all cheese sauce ingredients, except nutritional yeast in water about 25 minutes or until very soft.

3. Blend cooked ingredients with nutritional yeast in a high speed blender, until smooth. Salt & pepper to taste.

4. Place a tablespoon of steak mixture in the center of one egg roll sheet. Add a teaspoon of cheese sauce. Wet the four edges of the wrapper with water. Fold a corner diagonally over the mixture, then pull up the sides & corner to roll into a egg roll shape.

5. Place in frying oil that has reached 325 degrees. Allow to brown Remove from oil & drain. Let sit for 5 minutes before eating. Enjoy.

FINGER FOODS

There is always a need to have finger foods on the menu. I prepare finger foods for road trips, for parties, for retreats, for funerals, and for a night at home watching a movie.

A sit down dinner is not always optimal or preferred, so no worries. Put together some yummy finger foods and allow the crowd to graze, mingle, laugh, talk, and to keep things informal and easy.

SPINACH-STUFFED MUSHROOMS

Ingredients

20 medium sized white button mushrooms
1 TBSP vegan butter
3 cloves garlic, minced
4 cups fresh spinach, chopped
8 oz vegan cream cheese
4 slices of smoked vegan gouda cheese, room temperature
Salt, to taste
Pepper, to taste
¼ cup breadcrumbs

Instructions

1. De-stem mushroom caps.

2. Mince garlic, mushroom stems, spinach & sauté in vegan butter.

3. Lower heat and add smoked gouda cheese and vegan cream cheese, salt and pepper.

4. Stuff mixture into mushroom caps.

5. Sprinkle with bread crumbs and bake in a greased pan at 375 degrees Fahrenheit Fahrenheit for 12-15 minutes. Serve warm or room temperature.

GARLIC BUTTER "SALMON" CAKES

Ingredients

Garlic Butter
1 clove of garlic, minced
4 TBSP vegan butter
1 tsp of lemon pepper seasoning

"Salmon" Cakes
1 can of banana blossoms, chopped roughly
1 King Oyster mushroom, shredded with a fork
1 cup mashed potatoes
1 sheet of Nori ground finely
3/4 cup seasoned fish fry seasoning
Juice of 1 lemon
1 tsp of Old Bay seasoning
4 TBSP of vegetable oil for frying
Salt & pepper to taste

Instructions

1. Mix all ingredients together and form into patties.

2. Heat oil on medium high heat and fry patties well done. Drain on a paper towel

3. Melt vegan butter on the stove with minced garlic.

4. Brush patties with garlic butter sauce. Serves 4

SPINACH IN THE BLANKET

Ingredients

1 bag of fresh spinach, chopped roughly
3-5 large baby bella or white button mushrooms, chopped roughly
3 TBSP red onion, chopped finely
3 TBSP olive oil
8 oz vegan cream cheese
1 can of refrigerated crescent rolls, read the label to make sure they are plant-based
1 tsp sea salt (or to taste)
½ tsp freshly ground black pepper

Instructions

1. Sauté spinach, mushrooms, onions, in olive oil.

2. Let mixture cool and in a bowl, mix with vegan cream cheese.

3. Season to taste with salt & pepper.

4. Add a tablespoon of spinach and cream cheese mixture to one flat triangle of croissant.

5. Roll the croissant.

6. Place on a cookie sheet, 1 inch a part.

7. Bake until golden brown. Serves 4

"CHEESESTEAK" SLIDERS

Ingredients

Steak
4 Portabella mushrooms, sliced thin
1 small sweet onion, sliced thin
1/2 pint cherry, grape, or heirloom tomatoes, halved
2 cloves of garlic, minced
4 TBSP of vegetable oil for frying
½ tsp oregano
Salt & Pepper to taste

"Cheese Sauce"
3 small carrots
1 medium potato
1 small onion
2 cloves of garlic
½ tsp smoked paprika
1/4 cup of nutritional yeast
1/4 cup of plant milk
Salt and pepper to taste

Or

4 slices of packaged vegan smoked Gouda, room temperature

Slider Buns
12 vegan Hawaiian slider buns or French slider buns, read the label to make sure they are plant-based

Instructions

1. For Steak: Place sliced mushrooms, sliced onion, halved tomatoes, minced garlic, in a pan that has been coated with vegetable oil. These can also be roasted in the oven with 1 TBSP of oil if you don't want to sauté' or fry them. Fry them on medium heat or bake them at 375 degrees. Salt and pepper to taste. The mixture is ready when it is soft and caramelized.

2. For Cheese Sauce: Boil carrots, onion, & potato together. When tender, place into blender with plant milk, nutritional yeast, smoked paprika, garlic, salt and pepper. If the mixture is too thin, heat on the stove and stir until thickened. If it is too thick, add more plant milk. If you are using packaged cheese, place room temperature slices on top of warm steak mixture to melt it. Turn mixture until melted.

3. Assemble sandwiches: Separate the tops from the bottoms of the packaged buns, but do not separate the individual buns from each other. The bottoms should appear like a tray. Spread the steak mixture over the tray of bottoms, then pour the cheese sauce over the steak. Place the tops back onto the bread steak, and cheese tray. Then you can pull apart separate sandwiches. This methods keeps you from having to do the tedious task of making individual sandwiches. Drizzle plant-based butter over the top of the bread (optional). Serves 6.

SWEET GLAZED MEATBALLS

Ingredients

2 Beyond Burger patties, thawed
2 cloves garlic, minced (about 2 tsps)
1 TBSP shallots, minced
1 can black-eyed peas mashed
1/4 cup of plain bread crumbs
1 TBSP soy sauce, liquid aminos, or Tamari sauce
1 tsp cayenne pepper
4 TBSP maple syrup

Instructions

1. With gloved hands mix burger patties, garlic, shallots, mashed peas, bread crumbs, soy sauce and cayenne pepper.

2. Roll into balls and line them up on a greased cookie sheet to bake for 30 minutes on 375 degrees.

3. Remove from oven brush maple syrup over them and place back into the oven for 10 minutes.

4. Serve warm.

SANDWICHES

Your food path should lead you to what makes you happy. Do not allow guilt, other people's opinions or an over-arching food philosophy to stop you from enjoying what makes you feel amazing.

I am from New Jersey, so sandwiches were a staple growing up. Hot or cold, burger or sub, we ate some kind of sandwich everyday. I could probably do a cookbook on sandwiches all by itself.

Here are a few of my favorites. My only caution here is to read the labels on the breads you choose. Some breads have egg, cheese, and milk. If you are keeping it 100% plant-based, then read, read, read the label.

One more note about the labels. "may be made with milk or eggs" at the bottom of the ingredients list, usually means that the bread was made in a manufacturing plant with milk in it. If you do not see milk or eggs in the ingredient list, they were not put into the product. However, there could be the potential of cross-contamination from other products made in the same manufacturing plant. You have to make a personal choice if you are okay with items which may experience some cross contamination or not.

CHOPPED CHEESE SANDWICH

Ingredients

2 vegan hamburger patties (popular brands are Beyond, Impossible, Ultimate, Empower)
2 tsp of Adobo seasoning
5 mushrooms, sliced
½ small onion, sliced
1 TBSP mustard
1 TBSP ketchup
1 TBSP vegan mayo
1 TBSP of vegetable oil for frying
Salt & pepper to taste
1 sub roll
2 slices of vegan cheese, room temperature
1 lettuce leaf
4 tomato slices
1 chopped Pepperoncini pepper (optional)

Instructions

1. Place hamburgers, onions, & mushrooms on a flat grill on high heat. Allow one side of burger to brown and caramelize. Then flip to other side. Flip onions and mushrooms too.

2. Once both sides of the burger are caramelized, begin to chop the burger with the top of your spatula. Mix in mushrooms and onions (and peppers). Add in ketchup and mustard.

3. The chopped mixture should become one ground meat mixture. Shape meat into the shape of the sub roll.

4. Lay one slice of vegan cheese on top. Gently fold cheese into mixture until melted.

5. Cut open sub roll. Press into a panini press, George Foreman Grill, or place it on a flat grill with a pan on top. Remove when toasted.

6. Place meat mixture on the pressed bread. Lay lettuce and tomato. Press sandwich together, while tucking in ingredients. Cut in half. Serve Immediately.

VEGAN SLOPPY BURGER

Ingredients

2 vegan hamburger patties (popular brands are Beyond, Impossible, Ultimate)
1 large ripe tomato, sliced
1 ripe avocado
1/4 onion, sliced
5 baby bella mushrooms, sliced
1 fresh jalapeño, deseeded & sliced
2 TBSP vegan mayo
½ tsp garlic powder
½ tsp onion powder
Salt & Pepper to taster
2 slices of vegan gouda cheese or vegan pepper cheese
2 slices of vegan bacon
1 leaf of red lettuce
2 TBSP of oil for frying
2 TBSP of water
1 vegan Hawaiian Bun

Instructions

1. Place burger patties on an oiled hot flat griddle. Lower heat to medium. Add onions, mushrooms, and bacon to the pan.

2. Turn bacon and veggies often, so that they sauté gently. You want them to caramelize, but slowly so that they are soft and brown. You don't want burnt onions and mushrooms. Remove from pan once soft and caramelized.

3. Remove bacon from the pan after 1 ½ minutes on each side. Let drain on paper towel.

4. Flip burger patties once they are brown & caramelized on one side. Salt and Pepper. Add 2 TBSP of water to the pan, so that the burger remains moist while caramelizing.

Instructions

1. Add cheese slices that have been warmed to room temperature onto each burger patty. Turn heat to low and Cover with lid, so that cheese can melt. Be patient. Vegan cheese takes longer to melt.

2. Smash ripe avocado with a fork and mix in garlic powder, onion powder, salt and pepper.

3. Spread avocado on both sides of a grilled bun.

4. Add tomato to bottom of the bun. Then place your first burger patty with melted cheese on top.

5. Add bacon & sliced jalapeños. Then place your next hamburger patty with melted cheese on top.

6. Add grilled mushrooms & onions.

7. Add Fresh sliced onion (optional)

8. Add lettuce leaf.

9. Place top bun on.

10. The burger will be big and sloppy. You may want to cut it in half to eat.

11. Enjoy.

UNTUNA SALAD MELT SANDWICH

Ingredients

3 cups cooked chickpeas/garbanzo beans (1-28oz can) or two cups of dried chickpeas pressure cooked for 50 mins.
2 to 3 TBSP shallots, (or to taste)
2 to 3 celery stalks (approx. ½ cup)
2 TBSP relish
2 TBSP pimentos
2 mini sweet peppers, roughly chopped
2 TBSP ground Nori sheets, or Nori Komi Furikake
½ cup vegan mayonnaise (more if your prefer)
1 tsp sea salt (or to taste)
½ tsp freshly ground black pepper
1 package of smoked gouda vegan cheese, room temperature
1 loaf favorite vegan bread
2 TBSP vegan butter

Instructions

1. In a food processor pulse chickpeas, shallots. celery, relish, peppers, and pimentos.

2. Add the Nori flakes/Furikake rice seasoning, salt and pepper and mix to combine.

3. Add the vegan mayonnaise. Mix to combine and taste for seasoning.

4. Preheat oven to 300 degrees fahrenheit.

5. Butter bread slices and lay them out on a cookie sheet, butter side down.

6. Spread untuna mixture over bread slices.

7. Place room temperature vegan cheese slices over untuna bread.

8. Cover with foil and place in oven for 7 minutes. Bread should be light golden brown on bottom.

9. Remove foil. Add top layer of buttered bread, butter side up.

10. Switch oven to low broil and broil sandwiches for 3 minutes or until golden brown.

    *NOTE: Grind up one or two sheets of Nori (the kind used to make sushi) in a spice grinder. The mineral-rich Nori adds a nice "from the sea" flavor and look to the mixture. It is possible to use kelp flakes or dulse flakes too.

PORTABELLA "BEEF N' CHEDDAR" SANDWICH

Ingredients

Beef
4 Portabella mushroom tops
2 TBSP McKays beef bullion or ½ package of Recipe Secrets "beefy onion soup"
1 small onion
1 TBSP roasted garlic bullion
2 cloves fresh garlic, minced
1 cup of water
¼ tsp freshly ground black pepper

Cheese Sauce
1 medium carrot
1 medium potato
1 small onion
½ cup of raw cashews
4 TBSP nutritional yeast
1 cup of water
2 cloves garlic
4 vegan kaiser rolls or a vegan sub roll

Instructions

1. Slice Portabella mushroom caps very thin on a mandolin slicer.

2. Combine 1 cup of water, garlic cloves, onion, bullion & pepper in a saucepan to boil.

3. Place sliced mushrooms into boiling broth for 2-3 minutes. Mushrooms should be wilted. Remove and set aside.

4. Make cheese sauce by boiling carrot, potato, onion, cashews, and water until veggies are tender.

5. Blend boiled veggies with nutritional yeast and fresh garlic until smooth.

6. Place mushrooms on bottom piece of bread. Pour cheese sauce on top.

7. Serves 4.

DESSERTS

Enjoy desserts. Desserts are fun. Life is too short not to have a bit of sweetness. However, remember that to eat to live requires moderation in all things.

These desserts are made of fruits and vegetables, so remember to tell yourself that while you indulge. Most of all, enjoy every bite!

SWEET POTATO PIE

Ingredients

3 large sweet potatoes, boiled
1 stick vegan butter, softened
1/2 cup brown sugar, not packed
2 cups of organic white sugar
1 can of coconut condensed milk
3 vegan eggs equivalent replacement (prepare according to package)
1 tsp ground cinnamon
1 TBSP lemon extract
1 tsp lemon zest
1 TBSP vanilla extract
1/4 tsp salt
2 tsp nutmeg
9 inch unbaked pie crust (made with vegetable oil).

Instructions

1. Preheat oven to 350 degrees Fahrenheit.

2. In a blender add hot sweet potatoes with butter until smooth.

3. Add remaining ingredients except crust; blend well.

4. Pour into pie shell. Bake 40 minutes or until golden brown.

HUCKLEBERRY COBBLER

Ingredients

4 cups fresh or frozen blueberries
1 cup organic sugar (maybe more or less according to taste)
1 TBSP cornstarch
2 tsp nutmeg & cinnamon mixture (according to your taste)
1/2 cup of vegan butter softened
1 cup organic confectioners' sugar
1 commercial vegan egg equivalent replacer (mix according to package)
1 cup self-rising flour
1/2 tsp salt
1/2 cup cornmeal
2 TBSP maple syrup
3/4 vegan buttermilk (3/4 plant milk/ 1 TBSP white vinegar)

Instructions

1. Preheat oven 375 F degrees.

2. In a large mixing bowl mix berries, sugar, cinnamon/nutmeg mixture, and cornstarch.

3. Pour into greased 11x7-in baking dish.

4. Cream butter, powdered sugar, egg replacement together.

5. Sift flour and cornmeal together and stir into creamed mixture with milk in small batches until well blended. Pour on top of berries in dish.

6. Bake at 375 degrees Fahrenheit for 30-45 mins minutes or until knife comes out smooth.

7. Brush with melted butter and maple syrup when it comes out of the oven.

8. Serve warm with vegan ice cream.

MAPLE BANANA BREAD

Ingredients

2 ripe bananas
1/4 cup chopped pecans
1/2 cup vegan butter, melted
2 cups self-rising flour
1/2 cup maple syrup
3 TBSP plant milk
4 TBSP organic sugar
1 tsp maple extract or vanilla extract
4 TBSP applesauce

Instructions

1. Preheat oven to 350 F degrees.

2. Lightly grease an 5x9 in" loaf pan.

3. Mash ripe bananas in a mixing boil.

4. Add maple syrup, applesauce, milk, and extract.

5. Mix well.

6. Sift in flour to banana mixture.

7. Pour mixture into greased pan and spread evenly.

8. Bake for 50 minutes or until brown and toothpick comes out clean.

9. Let cool for at least 10 minutes then cut and serve.

BANANA ICE CREAM

Ingredients

4 frozen bananas
2 TBSP Nuts
2 TBSP Nutter butter cookies pieces
2 TBSP Vegan mini-marshmallows
2 TBSP Dried fruit.

Instructions

1. Place frozen bananas in a high speed blender or food processor

2. Blend on ice cream setting or until bananas reach consistency of soft serve ice cream

3. Mix in by hand, nuts, Nutter butter, vegan mini-marshmallows, or dried fruit.

CRANBERRY & APPLE SAUCE

Ingredients

1 1/2 cups organic sugar
2 apples, with skin & diced
1 cup water
1 (12-oz.) package fresh cranberries

Instructions

1. In a small saucepan over low heat, combine sugar and water until sugar dissolves.

2. Add cranberries and cook until they burst, 12 minutes.

3. Fold in apples & cover with for 10 minutes.

4. Eat warm with biscuits or Refrigerate for 4 hours.

5. Serves 10.

BREADS

It would not be vegan soul food without some great bread. Bread is the kind of food that makes us linger and enjoy each other. Taking the time to slather on some vegan butter or homemade fruit spread is just what a family needs when taking the time to catch up on each other's lives.

These recipes are easy and quick. No need to stress, these will be on the table in no time. They are quick enough to add to any meal, while comforting to the soul.

SKILLET CORNBREAD

Ingredients

1 cup oat flour (grind uncooked oatmeal in a high-powered blender)
1/2 cup yellow cornmeal
3 tsp baking powder
1/4 cup organic organic sugar
1 cup plant milk
1/4 tsp salt
1 commercial vegan egg equivalent replacer (mix according to package)
½ cup of vegetable oil.

Instructions

1. Preheat oven to 425F.

2. Mix dry ingredients in a bowl. Add milk, vegan egg replacement, and vegetable oil, and mix well.

3. Coat a 10-inch cast-iron skillet with vegetable oil and place in the oven for about 15 minutes.

4. Remove cast-iron skillet and pour in cornbread mixture.

5. Reduce heat to 375F degrees and bake for 25 minutes.

6. Brush vegan butter over the top & serve warm.

VEGAN "HONEY" BUTTERMILK BISCUITS

Ingredients

2 cups flour
1/2 tsp salt
4 tsp baking powder
1 TBSP organic sugar
1/2 cup vegan butter, Plus 4 TBSP
2/3 cup plant milk
1 TBSP of apple cider vinegar
4 TBSP` Agave Nectar

Instructions

1. Preheat oven to 425° F.

2. Place apple cider vinegar inside of the 2/3 of plant milk set it aside.

3. Put flour, salt, baking powder, and organic sugar into a bowl and mix.

4. Cut in the 1/2 cup vegan butter until mixture resembles course meal or pebbles.

5. Add plant milk mixture all at once and stir until dough forms a ball around the fork.

6. Turn dough onto a lightly floured surface and knead 14 times.

7. Lightly roll dough until 1/2" thick and cut with a biscuit cutter.

8. Spray cookie sheet and place the cut out biscuits onto it so they touch.

9. Bake 15 - 20 minutes or until golden.

10. Heat agave and 4 TBSPs of vegan butter together. Brush over biscuits.

11. Serves 12.

SIDES

Life is all about trying new things. No better way to do that, than to try a new vegetable, herb, or spice. Allow yourself to grow and to fall in love with vegetables again.

When you have great sides, main entrees are not always needed. I love sides. I often eat a dinner of all sides. I hope you enjoy my family favorites. There are some vegetables in my side dishes that you may not want to try, but do it. Try out my recipe and see if you fall in love with veggies like okra, turnips, and broccoli.

TURNIP GREENS

Ingredients

1/4 cup extra virgin olive oil
1 large onion, minced
5 cloves garlic, minced
2 pound turnip greens, chopped
2 white turnips, peeled and diced
2 TBSP of mushroom seasoning
2 large tomatoes, chopped
5 mini sweet peppers, minced
1 tsp liquid smoke
3 celery stalks minced
2 shallots chopped
Salt and freshly ground black pepper

Instructions

1. Mince all veggies except greens and turnips in a food processor.

2. Finely chop turnip greens leaves and stems.

3. Take the processed veggies and place into a stock pot or pressure cooker with olive oil. Sauté on medium heat.

4. Slowly add in chopped greens.

5. Cover the greens with sautéed veggies. Liquid will start to form on the bottom.

6. Slowly add in more greens & keep stirring. Add salt to allow more water to draw out of the veggies.

7. Cover with lid and cook with low pressure for 12 minutes or cook with covered lid for 30 minutes in a stock pot.

8. Remove lid once pressure had dropped or after 30 minutes, if using a stock pot.

9. Add in chopped turnips on top of greens.

10. Let steam for 5 minutes if using pressure cooker. 20 minutes for stock pot.

11. Serves 8.

GARLIC BROCCOLI

Ingredients

1 bunch of fresh broccoli broken into small florets
5 TBSP olive oil
1/2 tsp maple syrup
10 cloves chopped garlic
1/2 tsp Tamari sauce, organic soy sauce, or liquid aminos
1/4 tsp ground black pepper

Instructions

1. Steam broccoli for 3 minutes.

2. Remove from heat & let cool or rinse with cool water. It depends on how bright, green, & crunchy you want your broccoli. Cool water will keep them bright green.

3. Heat a large skillet over medium heat. Add the olive oil, maple syrup, Tamari sauce and garlic.

4. Add broccoli and stir. Add the salt and pepper, and continue to stir.

5. Coat broccoli thoroughly. Cook 5 minutes longer if you want very tender broccoli.

6. Serves 8.

CORN PUDDING

Ingredients

2 cups fresh corn (4-6 ears)
3 commercial egg replacers (according to package)
1 cup evaporated plant milk or 1 cup of full fat coconut milk
2 TBSP of vegan butter, melted
1 TBSP of organic sugar
3 TBSP flour
1 tsp salt & a dash of cayenne pepper

Instructions

1. Cut the corn off the cob into a medium bowl, but not all the way down to the base of the kernel.

2. Cut at about 3/4 way down so that you see corn milk after cutting the kernels.

3. Then scrape the corn milk off of the cob into the bowl.

4. Mix egg replacer according to package directions.

5. Whisk together milk, flour, egg replacers, melted butter, organic sugar, salt and pepper.

6. Pour mixture over corn, mix well in bowl.

7. Pour corn mixture into a greased 8 inch baking dish.

8. Bake at 350 for 45 - 60 min. and serve.

9. Serves 8.

FRIED CABBAGE AND POTATOES

Ingredients

1 head of cabbage, roughly chopped
3 TBSP vegetable oil
1 large onion, sliced
4 potatoes, sliced and peeled
salt and pepper, to taste

Instructions

1. Heat oil in a large skillet on medium-high heat, add onions and potatoes.

2. Season with salt and pepper & allow to lightly brown.

3. Add in the chopped cabbage, season again with salt & pepper.

4. Mix potatoes, onions, cabbage together in pan until cabbage is tender and lightly brown.

5. Serves 6.

BLACK BEANS AND RICE

Ingredients

3 cloves garlic
1 cup white onion
1/2 cup cilantro
1/2 cup sweet bell pepper (red, yellow, or orange)
1 small can of tomato & jalapeños
1 TBSP oil
1 15 oz can black beans drained or 2 cups of black beans which have been pressured cooked.
2 cups of uncooked parboiled brown rice
3 cups vegetable broth
1 TBSP of Sazon
Salt to taste

Instructions

1. Chop garlic, onion, cilantro, and peppers in a food processor or chopper.

2. In a heavy pot with a lid, heat oil on medium. Add mixture and cook for 3 minutes.

3. Add can of tomato cook another minute. Stir in rice and blend well.

4. Add black beans, broth, Sazon, taste liquid for flavor.

5. Mix well. Add salt to taste.

6. Reduce flame to medium-low, cover, and let water boil down until it is mostly absorbed.

7. Turn off flame and leave covered for 20 minutes without stirring or lifting the lid. The steam will cook the rice.

8. Serves 6.

STEWED OKRA, CORN, & TOMATOES

Ingredients

1 pound frozen or fresh okra
1 large onion, diced
1 tsp granulated garlic powder
3 mini-sweet peppers, diced
1 tsp smoked paprika
1 TBSP mushroom seasoning
Salt and pepper to taste
1 28 oz can fire-roasted diced tomatoes, do not drain
2 cups fresh cut corn
1 TBSP organic sugar

Instructions

1. Cut the corn off the cob into a medium bowl, but not all the way down to the base of the kernel.

2. Cut at about 3/4 way down so that you see corn milk after cutting the kernels.

3. Then scrape the corn milk off of the cob into the bowl.

4. In a skillet, gently sauté' onions & peppers until soft.

5. Add in corn & tomatoes.

6. Season with paprika, garlic powder, mushroom seasoning, salt & pepper.

7. Add organic sugar to taste.

8. Cook for 10 minutes

9. Serves 6.

SWEET POTATO SOUFFLÉ

Ingredients

Soufflé
5 sweet potatoes
½ cup plant butter or margarine
1 1/2 tsp vanilla extract
2 vegan eggs (Neat, Follow Your Heart) 1/2 cup plant milk
1/8 tsp salt
1 cup organic white sugar

Topping

1/2 cup flour
1 cup chopped pecans
1/2 cup sweetened coconut flakes
1 cup brown sugar
½ cup plant butter or margarine

Instructions

1. Preheat oven to 350 degrees Fahrenheit. Lightly oil a 2 quart casserole dish.

2. Scrub skin of sweet potatoes and boil in salted water. Cook until tender, 20 to 25 minutes.

3. Cool & peel potatoes.

4. Add potatoes, a stick of butter, vanilla extract, and egg replacements, salt, and organic sugar into a bowl.

5. Mix with electric mixer until smooth.

6. Place mixture into prepared casserole dish.

7. Combine pecans, coconut, brown sugar, a stick of butter, and flour.

8. Spoon mixture evenly on top of sweet potato mixture.

9. Bake for 40 minutes. Allow to set for 10 minutes.

10. Serves 6.

ENTREES

Try my converted favorites and get your whole life on a plate. It's a matter of your self-care.

These are favorites that I grew up eating, and that I had to learn to veganize once I gave up meat. There is no need to give up the things you enjoy just because you have given up meat and animal products.

SALISBURY STEAK

Ingredients

Steak
4 Beyond burger patties
1 small onion
1 shallot
2 garlic cloves
3 mini-sweet peppers, diced
½ cup bread crumbs
½ cup ground walnut
1 TBSP grill seasoning
Salt and pepper to taste

Gravy
1 large onion, sliced
4 TBSP vegetable oil
4 TBSP flour
1 TBSP mushroom seasoning
1 cup of water
½ tsp browning sauce

Instructions

1. In the food processor, finely mince onion, garlic, shallot, peppers and walnuts.

2. Mix by hand, burger with minced nuts and veggies.

3. Add in bread crumbs, grill seasoning, salt and pepper.

4. Form mixture into 6 - 8 patties.

5. Fry patties in oil. Brown both sides and remove from pan.

6. Leave oil in the pan and scrape up any fried bits from the patties.

7. Add sliced onions. Sauté until translucent.

8. Sprinkle flour onto onion and stir. It should begin to make a paste from the oil that is in the pan.

9. Mix mushroom seasoning with water & pour over flour paste.

10. Whisk continuously until smooth.

11. Add browning to make gravy brown.

12. Add patties into the gravy and simmer for 5 mins on low.

13. Serves 6.

GYRO SALAD

Ingredients

Gyro Meat
2 Beyond or Impossible Burgers
1 onion
2 garlic cloves
2 tsp granulated garlic
1 tsp cumin
½ tsp ground rosemary
½ tsp thyme
½ tsp oregano
4 TBSP tahini
Salt and pepper to taste
2 TBSP of vegetable oil

Salad
4 handfuls of mixed greens
1 large tomato, sliced and quartered
3/4 of english cucumber, sliced
½ sweet onion or red onion, sliced thin
3 TBSP vegan feta

Tzatziki Sauce
2 cloves garlic
Juice of one lemon
½ cup soaked cashews
½ cup plant milk
1 shallot
½ cup vegan sour cream
1/4 english cucumber
salt & pepper to taste

Instructions

1. In the food processor, finely chop all gyro meat ingredients, except the oil. It should look like a thick paste.

2. Form the patties from the paste and fry them in a pan with 2 TBSP of oil until browned on each side.

3. In a blender, add plant milk, vegan sour cream, ½ shallot, 2 garlic cloves, and lemon juice. Blend until smooth.

4. Slice cucumber and shallot very thin. Add into sauce and salt and pepper to taste.

5. Lay the bed of spring mix onto a platter. Spread the salad ingredients on top. Then add gyro meat and Tzatziki sauce.

6. Serves 6.

VEGAN CHILI

Ingredients

1 ½ cup walnuts, chopped
1 cup baby bella mushrooms, chopped
1 medium onion, chopped
4 cloves of garlic, minced
1 jalapeño, minced
4 mini peppers, minced
1 (10 ounce) can chopped tomatoes & chili (Rotel or a similar brand)
1 (28 ounce) crushed tomatoes
1 (28 ounce) can diced tomatoes
2 (16 ounce) Kidney beans
2 (16 ounce) black beans
2 (16 ounce) navy beans
5 TBSP olive oil
5 TBSP chili powder
1 TBSP granulated garlic
1 TBSP smoked paprika
½ TBSP cumin
1 TBSP onion powder

Instructions

1. Chop walnuts and mushrooms in the food processor until it resembles burger.

2. Sauté walnut mixture in a saucepan until brown, and liquid evaporates out of mushrooms. If you are using your pressure cooker, use the cooker liner to sauté ingredients.

3. Add finely chopped onion, garlic, peppers into sauté. Allow to become translucent. If you are not using a pressure cooker, transfer to large stock pot.

4. Add in cans of tomatoes, chili powder, garlic powder, onion powder, cumin, and paprika. Mix well. Bring to a boil if you are using a stock pot.

5. Add cans of beans. Do not drain. Mix well, and lower heat to a simmer. If using a pressure cooker, place lid on and lower heat.

6. Cook on low in a pressure cooker for 25 mins. In a stock pot, cook on low for 1 hour, stirring occasionally.

7. Serves 8.

VEGAN OXTAILS

Ingredients

1 cup vital wheat gluten
1 can of black-eyed peas, drained
1 small onion, chopped
5 garlic cloves
1 TBSP steak sauce
1 TBSP Tamari sauce
1 TBSP granulated garlic
1 tsp ground bay leaves
1 tsp ground thyme
1/4 tsp pink salt
1/4 tsp ground black pepper
1 package of onion soup
1 TBSP McKays beef bullion seasoning
3 drops liquid smoke
2 TBSP mushroom seasoning
1 king oyster mushroom, shredded with a fork
3 stalks celery
4 rice paper wrappers

Braise Sauce
1 parsnip
1 large onion
2 large potatoes
4 carrots
5 pressed garlic cloves
Salt & pepper to taste
3 TBSP chopped fresh parsley
1 TBSP rosemary, fresh
1 8 ounce can of tomato sauce
3 TBSP mushroom seasoning
1/4 cup red Wine, dry
2 TBSP McKays beef bullion seasoning
4 cups water

Instructions

1. Blend can of black-eyed peas, onion, garlic cloves, steak sauce, Tamari sauce, granulated garlic, bay leaves, thyme, salt, black pepper, onion soup, beef bullion, liquid smoke, and mushroom seasoning. This should be a very intensely flavored bean mixture.

2. By hand mix, shredded mushrooms, bean mixture with vital wheat gluten. Knead for 4 minutes.

3. Dip rice paper in warm water until soft and pliable.

4. Lay out rice paper and spread vital wheat gluten flat to cover the middle.

5. Place the celery stick down the center of the vital wheat gluten, as though it were a center bone of an oxtail.

6. Jelly roll the rice paper, vital wheat gluten, and celery until it forms a log.

7. Wrap the log in plastic wrap very tightly, and refrigerate for at least 24 hours.

8. After refrigeration, cut 2 ½ inch thick slices.

9. Brown the slices on each side in a fry pan with oil.

10. In a 3 quart pan with lid Bring to a boil all the ingredients in the braise sauce.

11. Place oxtails in braise sauce. If the liquid covers the oxtails, remove some. The liquid should come halfway.

12. Place pan in the oven with oxtails in braise sauce for 90 minutes at 375 degrees Fahrenheit.

13. Serve over rice.

14. Serves 4.

EGG FOO YOUNG

Ingredients

1 bottle of Just Egg
1 TBSP Tamari sauce
½ TBSP dark soy sauce
1 TBSP asian chili sauce
½ tsp Chinese 5 spice
½ cup shredded cabbage
½ cup sliced mushrooms
3 sliced green onions
½ cup bean sprouts
½ cup sweet pepper, shredded
½ cup shredded carrots
1 TBSP vegetable oil
Salt & pepper to taste

Brown Gravy
1/4 cup cornstarch
1 cup water
1 TBSP mushroom seasoning
1 tsp browning sauce
2 tsp Tamari sauce

Instructions

1. Mix Just Egg, Tamari sauce, dark soy sauce, chili sauce, Chinese 5 spice together thoroughly.

2. Add in vegetables.

3. Add vegetable oil to a fry pan. Heat on medium high heat.

4. Use a 1/4 of a cup mixture to pour patties into the fry pan. Allow the patties to brown on each side. It should take about 3-4 minutes on each side. Remove and set aside.

5. To make gravy. Whisk together all gravy ingredient s cornstarch and water.

6. Add mixture to pan that you removed the patties from. Whisk on medium heat.

7. Add browning sauce, Tamari sauce, and mushroom seasoning.

8. Whisk until smooth and a gravy consistency.

9. Add patties into the gravy.

10. Serve with rice.

11. Serves 4.

JACKFRUIT POT PIE

Ingredients

2 cans of young green jackfruit in water or brine,
24 ounces of mini potatoes or fingerlings, cut into bite size pieces
1 small bag frozen peas
2 medium onions, quartered
4 large carrots, peeled & cut into bite sized pieces
10 baby bella mushrooms, quartered
2 King Oyster mushrooms, shredded with a fork
2 garlic cloves, minced
1 sprig of fresh thyme
1 sprig of rosemary
1 cup dry red wine
2 ½ cups of water
2 TBSP mushroom seasoning
2 TBSP unbeef bullion (McKay's is a good one)
2 TBSP flour & 1/4 cup water to make slurry
3 TBSP olive oil
Salt & pepper to taste
Prepared vegan deep pie crust
Prepared puffed pastry dough (Pepperidge Farm is usually vegan)

For Filling

1. Soak jackfruit in a large pot of water for 20 minutes, if you were not lucky enough to find young green jackfruit in water. If you found it in water, no need to soak.

2. Sauté onions and garlic with 3 TBSP of olive oil.
    a. Pressure cooker/instant pot method: sauté in pot on sauté high setting.
    b. Slow cooker method: sauté on medium in a sauté pan.
    c. Oven method: sauté in deep, oven-safe sauté pan that is at least 4.5 quarts.

3. Add potatoes, shredded king oyster mushroom, and jackfruit to your sauté. Allow to lightly brown.

   a. Slow cooker method: transfer sautéed ingredients into your slow cooker and add carrots, baby bella mushrooms, red wine, water, mushroom seasoning, unbeef seasoning, fresh thyme & rosemary sprigs, salt & pepper. Slow cook on low for 6 hours or high for 3 hours.

   b. Pressure cooker/instant pot method: Add carrots, baby bella mushrooms, red wine, water, mushroom seasoning, unbeef seasoning, fresh thyme & rosemary sprigs, salt & pepper. Switch setting from Sauté to pressure cooker low. Cook on low for 12 minutes.

   c. Oven method: Add carrots, baby bella mushrooms, red wine, water, mushroom seasoning, unbeef seasoning, fresh thyme & rosemary sprigs, salt & pepper. Cover lid and bake on 350 degrees Fahrenheit for 2 hours.

For Pie

1. Slow cooker method: Add frozen peas and slurry to mixture.
   a. Transfer filling into deep pie crust.
   b. Cover with prepared puffed pastry dough. Cut vents in crust.
   c. Bake on 375 degrees Fahrenheit for 35 minutes or until crust is golden brown.

2. Pressure cooker/instant pot method: Allow pressure to release. Add frozen peas and slurry to mixture. Let mixture cool enough to handle without burning yourself.
   a. Transfer filling into deep pie crust.
   b. Cover with prepared puffed pastry dough. Cut vents in crust.
   c. Bake on 375 degrees Fahrenheit for 35 minutes or until crust is golden brown

3. Oven method: Add frozen peas and slurry to mixture.
   a. Transfer filling into deep pie crust (optional)
   b. Cover with prepared puffed pastry dough. Cut vents in crust.
   c. Bake on 375 degrees Fahrenheit for 35 minutes or until crust is golden brown

Serves 6.

BEYOND VEGAN RIBS

Ingredients

2 Beyond burgers, thawed
1 king oyster mushroom, shredded
½ can of young green jackfruit, shredded
2 mini peppers
1 celery stalk
½ medium onion
½ jalapeño, deseeded & deveined
2 garlic cloves
1 tsp grill seasoning
1 tsp granulated garlic
1 tsp onion powder
3 drops liquid smoke

Instructions

1. In a food processor mince all veggies, except mushrooms & jackfruit.

2. Add shredded mushrooms, jackfruit, & minced veggies to the thawed Beyond Burgers.

3. Mix well with your hands. Mixture should have lots of texture.

4. Place on a cookie sheet and press out to 2 inch thickness. Shape into a rectangle.

5. Score rectangle into rib like strips (about 2 inches wide).

6. Place in oven for 350 degrees Fahrenheit for 1 hour.

7. Remove from oven. Slather barbecue sauce on top & place back in oven for 10-20 minutes depending on whether you want it saucy or caramelized.

8. Serves 4.

FROM THE AUTHOR

As a minister of mind, body & Spirit, it is important to me that food nourishes the body, keeps the mind alert, and soothes the soul. Vegan soul food is my answer to finding that kind of food. In my opinion, eating plant-based food is the healthiest way to go. It keeps the mental channels clear, it allows your body to feel light and free, and when it tastes good, the Spirit delights.

Eating to live does not have to be boring. Eating soul food does not have to be unhealthy. It is possible to choose foods as a means of self-care. These dishes are meant to comfort your soul and your belly. They are meant to nourish your mind, body, and Spirit.

These are homestyle and down-home favorites which I have prepared for my family, friends, and other people whom I love. Some are new, some I have been bringing to the table for decades.

If you have ever attended an event, a retreat, a gathering, or a class where I have offered my culinary delights, you will always walk away remembering the food. Food is one of my many offerings. It means a lot to me to prepare a meal for people that I care about.

It is my desire that you will be able to offer these recipes of care and healing to your loved ones. But not only that, I want you to sit down and enjoy what you have created as a means of your own self-nurturing, and self-love. Enjoy!

Made in the USA
Monee, IL
16 September 2022